Eric Maldonado

THE FEARLESS WEALTH PLAN

A Simple Guide to
Achieving Your Financial Goals
Without Losing Sleep

THE
Short Book Formula
PUBLISHING

Eric Maldonado

Published by
The Short Book Formula Publishing

DISCLAIMER:
This book contains the opinions and ideas of the author. Careful attention has been paid to ensure the accuracy of the information, but the author cannot assume responsibility for the validity or consequences of its use. The material in this book is for informational purposes only. As each individual situation is unique, the author disclaims responsibility for any adverse effects that may result from the use or application of the information contained in this book. Any use of the information found in this book is the sole responsibility of the reader.

CONTENTS

INTRODUCTION

THE FEAR THAT STEALS WEALTH

My grandmother, Zulema Maldonado, was my favorite person. She was one of the kindest, toughest, most beautiful people I've ever known. She raised ten children, worked harder than most, and managed to pay off her house in full. Her home represented years of stability and security for our family.

Then she lost it.

Not due to a natural disaster or a market crash but through a couple of small financial decisions that compounded over time. She was so generous, always willing to help people in need. She took out loans against her paid-off house without fully understanding how the debt would work against her over time. She kept her financial decisions private.

As a nine-year-old, I remember a man in a suit showing up at our house with a briefcase. After he left, everyone seemed upset. Then the house was gone, lost to foreclosure, and we had to move.

That experience planted a question in me. What if she had someone to talk to about financial decisions from the beginning? Not salespeople pushing products, but a trusted guide who could have helped her avoid mistakes and make financial decisions in her best interest.

That's the work I do now as a financial advisor, and it's a big reason why I wrote this book.

THE REAL ENEMY ISN'T WHAT YOU THINK

After years of working with people who have significant wealth, whether from an inheritance, a business sale, retirement accounts, or insurance settlements, I've learned that the biggest threat to your financial future isn't market crashes, inflation, or even bad investment choices.

It's fear.

Fear causes people to make financial decisions in isolation. It causes people to have a scarcity mindset. Fear makes intelligent people keep too much money sitting in cash. It makes successful people sell all their investments at the very bottom of a bear market. It makes you second-guess yourself constantly. Fear causes you to go all-in and buy the speculative investment after it has already peaked.

The cruel irony is that decisions driven by fear, the ones that feel safest in the moment, are often the most dangerous to your long-term financial security.

This pattern plays out differently for everyone, but the underlying dynamic is awfully consistent. When you're afraid, you either freeze, keeping everything in cash and unable to make any decision. Or, you panic and make hasty decisions, selling at the worst possible time or jumping all-in on investments that have already run-up. Neither response serves you well.

Fear is unavoidable, but learning to work through it makes us stronger.

LEARNING TO MOVE THROUGH FEAR

From my own battles with fear, I know it can't be outsmarted, outflanked, or fully avoided. The path forward is through it.

The same is true in investing. The market will drop, sometimes violently. If you're invested in stocks, you'll likely experience spells where your account drops by a third or more. This isn't just a possibility; it's something that has happened many times and will most likely happen many times more. Conversely, when an investment idea or market sector becomes overly popular and reaches a fever pitch, there's a strong temptation to significantly over-allocate our portfolio to it, driven by the fear of missing out (FOMO). Even though this is when it is least valuable, all the gain has already been baked in.

The way to build lasting wealth is to stay invested through the downturns and staying diversified when the market bubbles up into one hot sector. Own shares in quality, publicly traded companies, diversified across categories and global regions, and hold them through scary times and times of irrational exuberance. Stay patient and disciplined when instincts tell you to run for cover and move all your investments to cash or to concentrate all your assets into the investment craze of the day.

This is where most people fail, not from picking wrong investments, but from letting fear drive them away from their plan at precisely the wrong moment.

WHY I WROTE THIS BOOK

I'm not writing as someone who's never made a financial mistake or never felt the fear of losing everything or the fear of missing out on making a killing on one perfectly-timed trade. I'm writing as someone who understands that successful investing is more about managing emotions and behavior than finding the one perfect investment.

I'm also writing as someone who believes work is good, we're uniquely designed to create value in the world, and financial freedom isn't only about accumulating more and more money. It's about having the margin in your day and in your finances to live according to your values, to be generous, to say "yes" to opportunities that matter most to you without being hindered by indecision or procrastination.

After seven years of building my advisory practice, my wife, Shelby, and I took our four children and spent a year in the mountains at Hume Lake, CA. It was a sabbatical we'd planned for from the start of the business, a time to rest, recharge, and spend extended time together as a family before digging into growth mode again. People asked if I was nervous about it. Of course I was. Was this a good idea? What if we get stuck on the mountain in a snowstorm? Would we regret moving twice in two years? Would my business continue to grow upon returning? Would the kids like it?

We'd built enough margin into our financial plan to make the choice, but we still had to trust that it would all be worth it in the end. We tried our best to focus on the goal from the beginning. That's what financial freedom looked like for us, not just saving money for the sake of having it, but having the option to make choices aligned with our highest priority.

That year was a real gift. The whole family loved it. My kids had a ton of fun on the lake and in the snow. Shelby loved the slower pace of mountain living. We made great family memories and new friends. And when we came back home, the business was still ready to grow again. It also had its challenges. It was a heavy lift moving back into a new home upon returning to the California central coast. But in the end, we got to see our shared goal come to fruition. Our family got to spend lots of time together enjoying the great outdoors. That made it all worth it.

I want that kind of freedom for you, too. Not necessarily a year in the mountains but whatever matters most to you. Whether that's retiring early, helping your grandkids with college, traveling, being debt-free, or just sleeping soundly at night knowing you have a plan that's working.

WHAT THIS BOOK IS REALLY ABOUT

This isn't another book about how to pick stocks or how to avoid a recession. I don't promise to predict the next bear market or to help you avoid market corrections. Anyone who makes those promises is either deceptive or deluded.

Instead, this book is about learning to invest fearlessly, which is something more fundamental and more difficult.

It means understanding that investing money in high-quality, publicly traded companies and holding them for the long term gives you a great chance of staying ahead of inflation and building lasting wealth. It means knowing that stock price drops are normal and even necessary. It means experiencing the wild swings in the stock market is the cost of admission for earning better returns over decades. It means having someone in your corner who can talk you through the moments when you want to panic and sell everything, or to capitulate and move all in on the one hot stock that everyone is clamoring about.

There's a story in the Bible about the prophet Elijah. He's hiding in a cave, terrified and alone. God tells him to stand on the mountain because He is about to pass by. First comes a wind so powerful it shatters rocks. But God isn't in the wind. Then comes an earthquake. But He isn't in the earthquake. Then comes a fire. But God isn't in the fire. After the fire comes a still, small voice. A gentle whisper. That's where Elijah finds God's presence.

That's what working with a trusted advisor can feel like during market turmoil. The financial world is shouting at you through the wind and the fire and the earthquake. The headlines scream catastrophe. Someone you know tells you a big recession is coming soon, and they sold all their investments to buy only gold and silver. The media amplifies every fear. But the still small voice comforts you.

An advisor can remind you, "We are prepared for this. We've seen this play out before. We know your values. We know your goals. Your investments are properly positioned. We are ready for this."

In the pages ahead, I'll share stories from my own journey and from clients I've worked with[1]. You'll meet Mary, who received a three-million-dollar insurance settlement after her father's passing and needed help learning to steward that wealth wisely. You'll meet a married nurse practitioner couple, Mark and Erin, who wanted their financial decisions to align with their faith and their calling. You'll meet people who were paralyzed by too much information, people who'd been burned by complicated products they didn't understand, and people who just needed permission to stop checking their accounts every day and to trust the plan.

Through these stories, you'll see how starting with values creates a foundation for making sound financial decisions. You'll learn why simple strategies almost always beat complex ones. You'll understand why having a guide who knows the terrain when the path gets scary is valuable.

WHAT YOU WON'T FIND IN THESE PAGES

This book isn't going to dazzle you with complicated stock-option tactics or promise you'll beat the market with a black-box investing scheme. I don't believe in those approaches, and I don't practice them with my clients.

1 Throughout this book, I've changed identifying details of client stories to protect privacy. Some stories are composites drawn from multiple similar situations. The principles and outcomes described are real, but the specific details have been modified.

I'm not anti-active-management or anti-advisory-fees. Good advice is worth paying for (I'm biased, obviously, as a paid financial advisor), and some people do well with actively-managed, dynamic-trading strategies. But I've found that for most people, especially those who've come into significant wealth and feel overwhelmed by the responsibility, simple is better. Set goals, build a plan, and implement an investment portfolio that gives you the highest probability of reaching those goals. Owning a diversified mix of the world's most valuable publicly traded companies, reinvesting the dividends, rebalancing regularly, and staying patient through market ups and downs has worked remarkably well for a remarkably long time.

I'm also not going to pretend this is easy. Staying invested when your account value drops by hundreds of thousands of dollars in weeks requires discipline, courage, and, often, an advisor who can remind you of the plan, show you how history has played out over time, and help you stay the course.

WHAT FEARLESS WEALTH *REALLY* MEANS

By the end of this book, my hope is that you'll feel equipped not just with good information but with the mindset and the tools needed to invest freely and confidently. To stop letting worry drive your decisions, to stop procrastinating or being burdened by more research and more information. To build a plan that works for your unique situation and then stick with it, even when headlines start to make you feel unsettled.

Because the truth is, it will get uncomfortable. Markets will spike and fall violently. You'll read scary predictions about the global economy. You'll hear about friends who made a lot of money on some investment craze you missed out on. But if you can learn to sit with that discomfort without acting in haste and keep moving forward even when fear pulls at you to jump ship, you'll be amazed at how much freedom and peace you can build.

That's what fearless wealth really means. Not the absence of fear but the courage to keep moving forward, anyway.

Let's get started.

CHAPTER 1

YOUR WEALTH JOURNEY STARTS WITH YOUR VALUES

WHEN I WAS COMPETING in high school wrestling, I had a simple but important ritual to write down my one big goal on my bedroom mirror. Every morning, I'd see my goal. "Become a State Placer."

When I got to college, wrestling Division I at Cal Poly in San Luis Obispo, my goals changed. Now my mirror displayed new targets. "Get a scholarship," and "Be the starting wrestler." These were my inspiration, the fixed points that guided my decisions. Every early morning run, every extra hour of practice when my body felt fatigued and sore, traced back to those goals on my mirror.

Amazingly, I was able to see many of those goals come to fruition. Not because I was more talented than my competitors, but because I had goal clarity (and by the grace of God!). I knew exactly what I was aiming for, and that focus gave me permission to say "no" to anything that didn't serve those goals.

Today, I use a similar approach with my clients as we're writing down what truly matters to them about money and life. And just as those goals on my mirror transformed my wrestling career, written values and goals transform how people invest and plan for their future. The written goals gave me focus when I wanted to quit. Written values and goals give my clients conviction when markets drop 30 percent or more, and they can't stop thinking about losing everything. Or, when they want to abandon the plan and go all-in on the one skyrocketing stock-of-the-day.

LESSONS LEARNED

In my first few years as an advisor, I made the mistake many financial professionals make by jumping straight into investing tactics. The conversations felt hollow. Clients would agree to the investment portfolio but lack the conviction to follow through. When the market experienced a correction of just 10 percent, they'd call me upset because we'd never established why they were investing in the first place.

Things changed when I discovered Bill Bacharach's values-based financial planning approach[2]. Instead of first asking about income and expenses or assets and liabilities, I learned to ask what matters most to them when it comes to their finances.

The first time I asked this question, I watched a successful business owner who'd built a multimillion-dollar construction company from zero pause and think. Nobody had ever asked him what he cared about most when it came to his money.

"My family," he finally said. "I want to make sure they're taken care of."

I asked why that mattered to him.

"Because I grew up with nothing. I was raised by a single mother, she worked incredibly hard, but we struggled. I never want my kids to feel financial insecurity."

He wanted his kids to have the options and freedom he didn't have and the ability to pursue a college education they felt called to.

Now we had something to build on. When the market dropped and he wanted to move to cash, I could remind him of what he had told me mattered the most. Did selling his investments at a loss move him closer to or further away from living out those values?

---

2 Bill Bacharach, *Values-Based Financial Planning: The Art of Creating an Inspiring Financial Strategy* (San Diego: Aim High Publishing, 2000).

Clarity of your values gives you an anchor when fear tries to sweep you away.

WHAT I HEAR WHEN I ASK "WHY?"

After hundreds of these conversations, I've learned that people's values tend to fall into a few broad categories, though each person expresses them uniquely.

SOME CLIENTS START WITH FAMILY. THEY WANT TO:
■ Make sure their family is planned for and provided for.
■ Have balance and enjoy time together instead of always working.
■ Travel as a family and create memories while everyone is still healthy.
■ Live close to grandchildren or aging parents and have the flexibility to visit regularly.
■ Leave a legacy for their kids or grandkids.
FAITH AND GENEROSITY SHOW UP FREQUENTLY:
■ Stewarding money well and honoring God with their resources.
■ Being generous and giving to causes that matter to them.
■ Supporting their church or non-profit organizations.
■ Helping the poor and needy.
■ Creating opportunities for the next generation.

Some clients simply say, "I just don't want to be stressed about money anymore. I'm tired of feeling behind on my financial goals, even though we make good money. I want to stop worrying and procrastinating about my financial future."

Others get more specific. "I want to buy a new fishing boat and get a black Labrador. I'd like to go to see my favorite rock band perform in England next summer. I want to go on epic trips with my wife while we're still young enough to enjoy them."

For me personally, freedom sits at the top. Freedom to spend time with my wife and our four kids. Freedom to take a family sabbatical-year in the mountains. Freedom to do work that matters, to give generously, to say yes to marriage anniversary adventure trips. When I'm at my best, that value of freedom has shaped our big decisions, from starting a business to homeschooling our children.

WRITTEN GOALS CREATE FOCUS

One married couple I work with, both entrepreneurs, told me their top value was "having balance and enjoying time with family." We wrote that down.

Six months later, the husband called about a business opportunity that would require double the travel time for at least a couple of years. This had significant upside career potential with a big increase in salary.

"Does it align with your values?" I asked.

Long pause. "We said balance and family time were our number one priority right now. This would be doing the opposite."

He passed on the job opportunity. Without that written value, he might have chased it and regretted it or passed and always wondered "if it was the right choice for my family and me."

WHAT HAPPENS WITHOUT CLARITY

I've had many meetings with prospective clients who rarely feel at rest or at peace with their financial decisions. These are engineers, doctors, and CEOs with successful careers, but they feel unsettled with their lack of financial planning.

One client told me about his brother, a lawyer making good money. For years, he's been looking for the right time in the market to pull the trigger and invest. He never feels like he can commit to something that will give him solace and confidence. He wants certainty that what he's doing is right, but there's always more information out there. Another newly uncovered opportunity that could change everything.

He's constantly flip-flopping, always feeling unsettled, moving in and out of investments. That's exhausting. Then the regret piles on top because he realizes if he'd just invested years ago into basic index funds based on his retirement date, he would have done so much better. Now he's fighting both the regret and the analysis paralysis, never truly feeling like what he's doing is right for him.

Without your own plan, you become vulnerable to whatever sounds good in the moment. Your neighbor made a killing in cryptocurrency. Your coworker's raving about a real estate deal they are doing. You hear that silver and gold are at all-time highs.

Real wealth gets destroyed by indecision and fear-based choices. Without a firm foundation, people constantly try to figure out where the market is going or what the experts online say they should be doing.

That's why we go back to values and make sure we're doing things that align with your unique areas of importance.

GETTING TO WHAT MATTERS THE MOST

When someone first sits down with me, I start simple. I ask, "What matters most to you? What do you care most about when it comes to your money?"

Sometimes people jump straight to numbers. "I want to retire at fifty-five with $5 million dollars in retirement accounts." That's a goal, which is good, but it's not the heart of the matter yet.

So I ask, "Why? Why is that important?" The purpose is to try to get to the deeper answer.

Maybe they say they want freedom from the daily grind. "Okay, why does that matter?" I ask. Maybe because they want more time with family. "Why is more time with family important to you?" Because they feel like they're missing their kids growing up. And further into their values we go.

It's not an interrogation. This isn't a survey or risk-tolerance questionnaire. I'm *genuinely* curious about their story, asking questions about their life, their background, and their family. That's how I get to know their values. I listen to learn what shaped them, what drives them now.

One prospective client came to me, a business owner, wanting to spend less time working. Through our conversation, we discovered that this was really about not repeating his father's mistakes. His dad had worked constantly, provided well financially, but they hadn't really connected. When his father died too young, he realized they didn't have a strong relationship. He didn't want that to be his story with his own teenage kids.

Now we're somewhere real. This isn't about hitting some magical retirement number at a certain age. It's being present with his kids now rather than just providing materially for them.

When we built his financial plan, we didn't just calculate how much he needed to retire. We looked at ways he could step back from the business sooner, perhaps hand off day-to-day operations while staying involved strategically. We structured things so he could be home for dinner, help coach his son's baseball team, and be present *now* instead of waiting for some future date that might never come.

Sometimes it's just a few minutes of me asking questions to get to a deeper answer. Other times it takes longer. During the meeting, I sometimes give examples of common values I've heard to help get them thinking. Examples include faith, family, freedom, security, flexibility, not being a financial burden on adult children, generosity, travel, or staying close to grandkids geographically.

Maybe they've not thought about it in these terms before. Maybe hearing their spouse share what matters most to them is new information. Clarity helps couples move forward together instead of pulling in different directions.

Once we write it down, it becomes real and tangible. It's now something we can build toward and check against when big decisions come up. It's something we return to when markets drop, and fear wants to take over or when there's a hyped-up investment fad we may be tempted to chase after. These values ground us to what's really important.

This process takes us from theoretical to meaningful, from surface conversation to what you care about most. Once we're operating at that level, dealing with market volatility or market euphoria becomes much easier to weather because there's an actual reason to stay the course beyond just wanting more money for the sake of having more.

VALUES AS YOUR INVESTMENT SHIELD

Having clarity about values functions as a shield during difficult market conditions. Not because values magically protect portfolios from dropping. They don't. But because when someone knows what they're working toward, panic becomes harder to justify.

Josh and Melissa[3] came to me wanting a better plan. Together, we identified their values and goals. Balance, time with family, living financially stress-free, traveling together, and seeing their parents through their golden years were their priorities. We made specifically written goals. They wanted to retire from full-time work in nine years, remodel the kitchen and bathroom by year-end for no more than $110,000, buy an electric vehicle in two to three years for around $35,000, take a family trip to Italy next year for a maximum of $15,000, and help fund their daughter's wedding with $20,000 saved by that time.

Then 2022 hit with high inflation, aggressive Federal Reserve rate hikes, Russia invading Ukraine, widespread recession fears, and markets tumbling. Both stocks and bonds were down simultaneously, which isn't supposed to happen.

---

3 Names and details have been changed to protect privacy. This example is for educational purposes only and does not represent any specific client or guarantee results.

Josh called, concerned. They wanted to move everything to cash, wait out the drop and the potential recession, then get back in when things felt safe again.

I pulled up their written financial plan on the screen during our Zoom meeting. "You said you want to retire from full-time work in nine years," I reminded them. "To have a realistic shot at your retirement income goals from your investments, you need to stay in growth mode. Markets experience a drop of 20 percent or more once every five or so years on average. This is part of the process, not a reason to abandon it."

I also pointed out that their ongoing retirement contributions were now buying at lower prices. Dollar-cost averaging was working exactly as designed.

They stayed the course, and I was so proud of them. It's not easy to go against your emotions.

The S&P 500 total return was down about 18 percent in 2022. The very next year, the total return was about 26 percent. By staying the course, they captured the upswing the following year instead of sitting in cash, watching it happen without them.

We met throughout the year to reconfirm values, goals, and action items, and to reconfirm that the portfolio could drop significantly at any given moment, but we are ready for that. I'd already laid the groundwork with their investment plan, the goals that drove the plan, and what they cared about most in life.

When the market dropped, we didn't need to figure out what to do. We'd already visualized it and thought about it. Now they just needed to execute what we'd trained for.

Values-based planning is not just a feel-good exercise. It's the difference between being too conservative with your investments and achieving what matters most to you.

FREEDOM THAT COMES FROM KNOWING

People with clear, written values experience a specific kind of freedom. Not necessarily freedom from ever worrying about money but freedom from constantly second-guessing themselves.

They can look at their accounts during a market downturn and feel concerned without panicking because they know their values haven't changed, and their strategy aligns with those values. They can hear about their friend's big investment win without feeling envious because they're on their own path toward achieving their own goals.

Your values give you the courage to act despite fear, to stay committed despite uncertainty, to trust the process even when your impulses tug at you to do something different.

For my own family, this played out dramatically during our sabbatical year. When doubts crept in, we went back to that written value and goal. It gave us permission to follow through even when fear suggested we were making a mistake.

That's the power of this foundation. Everything else in your financial life becomes simpler when you know what you're building toward and why it matters.

DISCOVERING WHAT MATTERS MOST

How do you discover and articulate your values? Here's what I do with clients in one of our first planning meetings.

FIRST, I ASK OPEN-ENDED QUESTIONS:
What matters most to you when you think about your finances?
What do you want to be doing most with your time?
What keeps you up at night when you think about money?
If money weren't an issue, how would you spend your days?

I listen. I ask follow-up questions. I dig into the "whys" until we hit bedrock.

I help clients write it down in specific language that means something to them, personally. We don't write, "financial security." We write, "having enough money that my daughter doesn't have to take out student loans like I did," or "being able to retire at sixty, so I can spend winters near my grandkids in Phoenix."

We create a living document with a list of your core values. In addition, we build out specific goals with dollar amounts and timeframes, the "why" behind each goal, and how you'll know you've succeeded. Then we review it regularly. At every meeting. When market conditions change. When life circumstances shift. We modify goals as needed. But the values tend to stay the same, as they are core to who you are and what you care most about.

CHAPTER 2

WHY LESS COMPLEXITY MEANS MORE WEALTH

I MADE A THREE-JAR piggy bank for my kids. It's literally just three jars taped together, nothing fancy. Each one has its own label written with a Sharpie: Give, Spend, and Grow. The Give jar is meant to teach them about being generous. The Spend jar is for toys, for the arcade, or whatever brings them joy. Currently, my son is using it to save up for an electric dirt bike. We don't call the last jar save; we call it grow.

Grow. That word matters. Saving is more akin to just burying your money. The money's purchasing power is eroding over time. Growing takes work. Growing takes ideas and ingenuity. Growing takes faith that what you plant today will be worth more tomorrow. Growing allows you to have the chance to beat inflation. For my kids, "grow" money could be used for things like starting a lemonade stand, making a craft to sell at a youth entrepreneur fair, or to help pay for a robotics camp they've been wanting to go to.

The same principle applies to investing. You want your money to grow, not just sit there. Most people get it backward because they think growing money requires the most complex, sophisticated approach they can find. The three jars concept worked for my kids because it was simple enough to understand and use every day. The same is true for building wealth. Simple beats complex almost every time.

Most of the financial industry wants you to believe the opposite. They want you to think that growing money requires complex products or sophisticated strategies. They profit from your confusion. The more complicated they can make investing seem, the more they can charge you to navigate that complexity.

But I've learned after fourteen years working in financial planning and eight years since starting my own firm that the boring stuff works best. Simple strategies outperform complex ones. Usually, if something is easy to do, it's also easy *not* to do, which is why so few people stick with what actually works.

Flossing. Exercising. Drinking water. We know these things are best for our health, but we still find ways not to do them. The same is true with investing.

THE COMPLEXITY TRAP

When I first started my financial advisory firm, I worked with a graphic design business owner in his thirties. He was married with young kids, had a successful company, and was paying thousands of dollars a year into a whole life insurance policy. He didn't know why he had it. When I asked him about the life insurance policy, he couldn't tell me how much death benefit he had. He didn't know how the cash value worked. He couldn't explain the dividends, the surrender charges, or when he could access the money.

"My friend set me up with this," he told me. "He said it was a smart way to save."

We spent an hour or so going through the policy together. The premium was costing him thousands of dollars a month. By the end, he was surprised to discover he had cash value funds that he had access to. The death benefit he was paying all that money for was something he could get with term insurance for a fraction of the cost. The cash value he'd built up over several years was less than the premiums he had paid in. No real growth. No real return.

We closed the policy, took the cash value to fund his emergency fund, bought adequate term life insurance, and set up tax-free Roth IRAs for him and his wife. Now he knows exactly where each dollar is going and why. He's on pace to reach his near-term and long-term goals. The complexity that seemed sophisticated was really just expensive confusion.

This happens all the time. People come to me with forty different investments in their accounts. Individual bonds they don't understand. Sector funds that overlap. Tactical strategies that promise to time the market. High-fee, actively-managed funds that are trying to guess where the market is going next.

One client had been with another advisor who had her in so many different holdings that she couldn't even read her statements. She didn't know what she owned or why. When markets moved, she had no idea if she was doing well or poorly because everything was so convoluted. She could never file taxes on time because it took forever to get the 1099 tax document in the mail.

"I just feel lost," she told me. "My advisor made it seem like all this complexity was necessary, but I don't understand any of it."

We simplified everything down to a handful of low-cost, diversified, index-based Exchange Traded Funds (ETFs) that each own hundreds of different companies. Companies in categories like US Large Cap, US Small Cap, International Developed Markets, Emerging Markets, and Global Real Estate. That's it. Now she understands precisely what she owns and why. Her investment fund fees were cut in half. Most importantly, her confusion disappeared.

THE CLARITY TEST

When someone tries to sell you an investment product, apply the clarity test. If you can't explain it to a twelve-year-old in two minutes, it's too complex.

Can you explain indexed stock ETFs to a kid? Sure. You own a small slice of hundreds of publicly traded companies. The index follows a basket of stocks like the S&P 500, which is comprised of 500 of the largest US companies. When they make money, you make money. Simple.

Can you explain a variable annuity with an enhanced death benefit rider? Good luck. I've been in this business for fourteen years, and I sometimes still need a manual to understand these products.

Complexity is a hiding place for higher fees. It's a smokescreen for poor performance and a way to make you dependent on the person selling it to you.

Simplicity is *transparency*. When you understand precisely what you own and why, you can make better decisions and stay the course.

THE PERMISSION TO BE BORING

Boring investing works. There's no need to chase the next big thing or impress anyone with complex strategies. Understanding every new financial product isn't necessary.

What's worked for over a century still works today, and that is owning productive businesses through simple, low-cost, diversified equity funds...many of which pay quarterly dividends. It's not exciting, but it doesn't need to be. Your *life* should be exciting. Your long-term investments can be boring and effective.

One client told me she wanted something simple. She'd been jumping from strategy to strategy for years, always feeling like she was missing something. We built her a "vanilla ice cream portfolio." Nothing fancy. No exotic flavors. Just solid, reliable, time-tested, equity-based, broadly diversified low-cost ETFs.

"This is the first time I've understood my investments in twenty years of working with advisors," she told me.

Another client loved the idea of simplicity so much that he said, "I feel like I can finally stop wondering if I'm doing the right thing."

That's the confidence that comes with clarity and simplicity.

THE AUTOMATION ADVANTAGE

Simplicity enables automation, and automation is one of the most powerful tools for building wealth. When your strategy is complex, you have to constantly monitor and adjust. When it's simple, you can automate more.

Monthly investments? Automated. Rebalancing? Set a date, and stick to it. Dividend reinvestment? Automatic.

Automation removes willpower and reminders from the equation. You don't have to remember to invest. You don't have to overcome the fear of buying when markets are down. You don't have to fight the temptation to stay overly concentrated in the hot sector.

It just happens.

I learned this as a wrestler. The moves that worked were the ones I'd drilled thousands of times until they became automatic. In the heat of competition, I didn't have to think. My body knew what to do.

Same with investing. Make it automatic, and you remove the opportunity for FOMO decision-making to interfere.

THE COURAGE TO KEEP IT SIMPLE

It takes courage to keep things simple in a world that offers more and more complexity.

It takes courage to say, "That's interesting, but I'm good with my plan." It takes courage to admit you don't understand something and therefore won't invest in it.

While others are jumping from investment idea to investment idea, paying transaction fees and taxes, and trying to time the market, you're quietly building wealth through compound growth in a diversified portfolio of equities that have real earnings growth and pay real dividends.

THE BOTTOM LINE

Complexity in investing is usually unnecessary, often expensive, and almost always a source of stress rather than success.

The financial industry doesn't want you to know this because simplicity would put a lot of people out of business. But this isn't about them. This is about you and your family and your future.

Expertise in stock derivatives, options, or private equity isn't required. Leveraged ETF strategies and margin loans aren't necessary. Paying high investment fund costs for rarely materialized market-beating returns doesn't make sense.

A simple strategy you can understand and stick with works best. Owning great businesses through basic, low-cost, publicly traded indexed ETFs provides growth potential and helps beat inflation. Confidence comes from understanding the story of what you're invested in.

In the next chapter, we'll talk about why even with a simple strategy, fear will still show up. Markets will drop, panic will set in, and every instinct will tell you to abandon your plan. Or, a single stock or commodity will go to the moon, and you'll be tempted to pile everything into it.

But you won't because you understand that fear of loss and fear of missing out are normal parts of investing, and we'll have strategies to face them.

The path to wealth isn't complicated.

The courage to stay on that path when fear strikes is where the real work begins.

CHAPTER 3

HOW EMOTIONS SABOTAGE YOUR FINANCIAL FUTURE

I WAS THIRTY YEARS old, driving on the 101 freeway through L.A. traffic in the afternoon, something I'd done many times before. Then suddenly, out of nowhere, it felt like the world was ending.

My heart started racing. My stomach tightened. The sky felt like it was falling. Every alarm in my brain was signaling that something was catastrophically wrong, even though nothing had changed around me.

I pulled off at the next exit and somehow made it to a Burger King parking lot. I sat there, trying to relax, praying, asking God for help. I ordered some food; maybe I was just hungry. I tried calling Shelby; it went straight to voicemail. I was on my own with whatever this was. Or so I thought.

I tried to get back on the freeway. The feeling started coming back. But by the grace of God, I just didn't stop. I kept going, kept driving forward, trying to get closer to home. I was still three hours away. After a while on the road, the intense feelings started to dissipate.

I got home exhausted, hoping it wouldn't happen again, but I didn't really know what it was.

Over time, I learned this was a panic attack. I shared about my experience with my wife and my friends. "Oh yeah, I've had one of those. I thought I was having a heart attack," a friend would say. People don't talk about panic attacks much, but once you realize what they are and start reading books and listening to experts who understand the triggers and responses, you become equipped to deal with those moments constructively. That doesn't make it easy, but it *does* give hope that you can overcome.

Even to this day, I still feel moments of fight-or-flight coming on, and I really have to focus on moving through the fear of the *feeling*. At a certain point, you're not really afraid of anything specific in front of you; you're more afraid of the feeling of panic itself. This disrupts your ability to function normally.

This experience taught me that, sometimes, your mind has to tell your brain what to do because your brain can get triggered by the fight-or-flight response.

Your mind, above the bodily response, has to be able to dictate your actions until the brain and gut can calm down.

Eventually, the feeling of panic ends. When it does, you don't want to regret the actions you took while feeling intense discomfort. You don't want to make permanent decisions based on temporary feelings.

The only way to gain freedom from the episode of angst is to enter those uncomfortable moments voluntarily. To get back in the car. To take the drive. To exercise courage. To bring people into the equation. I tell my wife and friends what I'm afraid of. I use resources to work on managing fear and panic. I have a plan, resources, and tools from people who know more than I do.

The lesson applies directly to investing because having someone to help makes a difference. Being honest about what you're experiencing matters.

In a panic attack, staying put and letting it take its course is how you get through it. Not trying to outrun it. You end up better on the other side. More confident. More free. With investing, you don't have to run from volatile markets all the time. You can move through those moments calmly.

THE TRUTH ABOUT FEAR

Feeling afraid of investing in the stock market is normal. In fact, if you're not occasionally exercising courage by sticking with your investments, you're probably not taking enough risk to keep up with the rising costs of a multi-decade retirement.

The problem isn't that we feel fear, but that we let fear make our decisions.

When I feel panic coming on while driving, the worst thing I can do is avoid driving altogether. The fear wins. The pattern gets reinforced, and my options become limited.

I have to keep driving, keep breathing, keep moving forward, even when every part of my body is shouting at me to turn back. Therapists call this exposure therapy. Successful investors do something similar.

Market fear can feel somewhat like a panic attack. It can trigger the same primal response to fight, flee, or freeze. Maybe not with the same intensity, but with similar avoidance results.

And just like with panic attacks, the only way to build wealth is to stay in the car (investments), and keep driving (trust the plan).

EMOTIONAL MISTAKES THAT DESTROY WEALTH

There are some expensive emotional reactions in investing.

THE PANIC SELL

MARKET DROPS OVER 25%

You sell everything to wait "until things calm down."

ANALYSIS PARALYSIS

WHEN THINGS FEEL "SAFE" THE MARKET HAS ALREADY RECOVERED

TOO LATE!

Locked in Losses, Missed the Rebound.

STUCK ON THE SIDELINES

— ALWAYS HESITATING...NEVER INVESTING.

THE OVERCONFIDENCE SURGE

OPPORTUNITY

Everything you touch turns to gold.

All-In on One Hot Stock!

CONCENTRATION RISK

ONE STOCK CRASHES 80%

FROM HERO TO ZERO
STAY DIVERSIFIED

First, there's the panic sell. The market drops over twenty-five percent, and you can't take it anymore. You sell everything and move to cash "until things calm down." By the time things feel calm, the market has recovered, and you've locked in your losses while missing the rebound.

Then there's loss aversion and the paralysis of analysis. You've been burned before; now you won't invest at all. You keep waiting for the perfect moment, enough information, the clear signal, the guarantee that this time will be different. That moment never comes.

Then there's the overconfidence surge. Everything you touch turns to gold. You're a genius. You concentrate everything into your best performer. Then it drops seventy percent, and you learn why owning a lot of different companies at the same time matters.

You might experience FOMO. Your neighbor made a fortune on Tesla stock. Your coworker's bitcoin paid for a new boat. Suddenly, your portfolio of diversified low-cost equity-based ETFs earning steady returns feels embarrassingly inadequate. You abandon your plan and chase the meme stock.

I've watched people blow up their entire retirement savings trying to catch the next Amazon or Apple stock, chasing a quick tenfold return. They'll take money that took decades to accumulate and gamble it on a feeling, a tip, or a fear of being left out of the next single-stock run-up.

I've seen every one of these emotions cost people hundreds of thousands of dollars. Smart people. Successful people. People who rarely make these mistakes in their professional lives somehow lose all rationality when it comes to their investments.

WHEN EVERYTHING FALLS APART AT ONCE

Mike[4] owned a coffee shop. He was in his mid-forties, a single parent with a son who had just graduated from high school and who also helped work in his cafe. The shop was everything to him.

Then, in March 2020, the state ordered all restaurants closed.

Mike's concern was that he would lose the restaurant and be destitute. "I'm not going to find a new job. I don't have a college degree. I put all my eggs in this one basket," he said. He was worried about himself, his son, and his employees.

His previous concerns about helping to pay for his son's college tuition or saving for his own retirement were now on the back burner. His income had stopped. His investments were dropping alongside the market crash. He was watching both sides of his financial life collapse simultaneously.

Business owners understand resilience because they live it. His cafe was a small business. The index funds in his portfolio owned hundreds of companies, each fighting to survive and adapt.

He didn't sell his investments to move to cash.

4 Names and details have been changed to protect privacy. This example is for educational purposes only and does not represent any specific client or guarantee results.

Instead, he pursued Paycheck Protection Program (PPP) loans and Small Business Administration (SBA) funding. He kept his staff together as best he could. When outdoor dining opened up, he built parklets on the street.

His portfolio dropped hard in March. But then it recovered.

His financial plan included a personal cash reserve and a business cash reserve. Together, they provided about eighteen months of cash for expenses in high-yield savings accounts that didn't fluctuate with the stock market. Those funds allowed him to wait out the loan-forgiveness process without touching his investments.

Through 2020 and into 2021, Mike dealt with ongoing stress. He had the PPP loans, but would they be forgiven? He had an SBA loan with better terms, but it was still debt. In 2021, it was hard to find staff available to work in food service. Inventory costs were soaring.

By late 2021, Mike's restaurant was recovering. Revenue was growing. The PPP loans were forgiven. The SBA loan turned out to be low-interest and long-term with a manageable monthly payment. He had a viable path to keep his restaurant running, make payroll, save for the future, and pay off the small-business loan with restaurant profits.

His investment portfolio had also recovered with the market.

Mike stayed invested throughout it all. By 2023, markets had recovered and pushed higher. His cafe was thriving. He's now helping his son with college expenses and funding his own retirement plan.

He used to check his investment account balances every single day. He'd see the balance drop by tens of thousands of dollars, and it didn't feel good. But he'd experienced enough of these drops to know it would eventually go back up.

It's okay to look at your accounts. It's okay to experience the emotional pain of seeing drops. But it's the acting on that fear and selling at a market bottom that causes the damage. He learned to feel the discomfort without letting it control his decisions. He's thankful he didn't move to cash after the initial drop, causing him to miss out on all the subsequent gains.

WHY WE'RE WIRED TO FAIL AS INVESTORS

Human beings are terrible investors by nature. We're pattern-seeking creatures who see trends where there isn't one. We're social beings who feel physical pain when we go against the crowd. We're survival machines programmed to run from danger, and market volatility feels dangerous.

These traits kept our ancestors alive in the wild, but they'll kill your portfolio.

Losing money hurts *more* than gaining money feels good.

When our ancestors saw everyone in the group running for their lives, those who stopped to see whether there really was a bear didn't make it. The ones who ran first and asked questions later survived to pass on their genes to the next generation.

Now flip that to investing. When everyone is selling in a frenzy and buying CDs and treasury bonds, your instincts demand that you run with them. But the ones who stop to breathe, remember that markets recover, and stay put despite the fear, are the ones who build wealth.

We're fighting human nature every time we stay invested during a market crash or stay diversified during a stock market bubble.

YOUR EMOTIONAL FIRE DRILL

Waiting until the crisis happens in order to figure out how you will handle it doesn't work. Just like we did fire drills as kids in school, you need to do emotional fire drills for your investments before the market catches fire.

That's why I consistently talk to clients about historical market drops. In our meetings. In my newsletters. We look at what has happened before, the likelihood that it will happen again, and what we'll do about it. Not *if* the market drops but when.

One client told me, "You talk about market crashes so much that when it finally happened, I was almost disappointed it wasn't worse."

That's the point. If you're prepared for a 50 percent drop, a 35 percent drop feels manageable.

THE COMFORT OF DISCOMFORT

There's a phrase therapists use that changed how I think about panicking. "It's uncomfortable but not dangerous."

When I'm driving and feel anxiety rising, I remind myself that this is uncomfortable, but I'm not *actually* in danger. My body is having an adrenaline response. I can keep driving and be all the better for it.

The same is true with investing. A one-third market crash is uncomfortable, but if you own well-capitalized, earnings-producing, dividend-paying companies through low-cost investment funds, you're not in real danger long term. The probability that hundreds, or even thousands, of large publicly traded companies all go to zero at the same time and stay there forever is incredibly small.

Watching your account value drop by tens or even hundreds of thousands of dollars feels terrible. But feeling terrible and *acting* on it are two entirely different things.

The mistake people make is treating discomfort as an inevitable danger. They sell to make the discomfort stop, not realizing they're creating real danger by locking in losses and missing recoveries.

That's when you need to hear the still small voice reminding you that this is uncomfortable but not dangerous. The more you stay invested through downturns, the more resilience you build.

THE PERMISSION TO FEEL AND GETTING STRONGER

When markets crash, it's normal to feel sick to your stomach. It's normal to question everything. It's normal to want to sell it all and hide out in cash.

Feel all of that. Talk about it. Call your advisor and say, "I'm concerned about this," or, "I'm upset about this. What are your thoughts?" Write in your journal about how much you hate seeing your account value drop.

Just don't *act* on those feelings by selling and moving to cash if your values and goals haven't changed.

There's a big difference between feeling fear and being controlled by it. You can be terrified and still stay invested. You can hate market volatility and still understand it's necessary. One of my clients looks at her account every single day. "I can't help it," she says. "But I rarely do anything about it. I just look, feel whatever I feel, and then go about my day." She's learned to separate feelings from actions.

Each time you stay invested through a downturn, you become more resilient. You build confidence in your ability to endure discomfort. The next drop feels a little less catastrophic. Even better, you start to see market drops as buying opportunities, since the market is on sale. You become what author Nassim Taleb calls "antifragile,"[5] someone who actually gets stronger through stress and volatility.

Panic attacks have made me stronger. I've become less fearful by having to face them. Now when they come, I'm ready. The same thing happens with market drops.

My college wrestling coaches understood this. Before big matches, they'd say, "You're going to get tired. Your legs will feel heavy. That's normal. That's your body getting ready." During matches, when I'd look over exhausted and sometimes behind on points, my coach wouldn't be frantic. He'd be calm. "Good job. Stay low. Keep attacking."

His calm became my calm. His confidence became my confidence.

That's what a good financial advisor does during market turbulence. We don't pretend it's not scary. We don't minimize your feelings. We don't make you feel foolish for showing concern. But we also don't add fuel to the fire of fear and worry. When you call us upset because the market is in a downturn, we're the still small voice that says, "I know this doesn't feel good. But we are ready for this. This is the cost of admission

---

5 Nassim Nicholas Taleb, *Antifragile: Things That Gain from Disorder*, Incerto (New York: Random House Trade Paperbacks, 2014).

for long-term returns. Your portfolio is properly positioned. Stay the course."

We lay the groundwork before the crisis. We look at the long-term historical results. We align your investment portfolio and financial plan with your values and goals. When the market drops, we're not scrambling to figure out what to do. We already know. We've already prepared. And we're welcoming any questions you may have along the way.

THE WEALTH TRANSFER MACHINE AND YOUR CHOICE

Warren Buffett said the stock market is a device for transferring money from the impatient to the patient. Every market crash is a money transfer event, but not the way most people think.

When markets drop and people panic-sell, they're transferring their future wealth to people who stay invested. Every share they sell in fear is bought by someone willing to endure the discomfort. During the COVID-19 crash, the fearful sold to the patient. During the 2008 Great Financial Crisis, the scared sold to the antifragile investors. Every time, patience has been rewarded, and fear has been punished.

The cruel part is that fear feels rational in the moment. When everyone around you is selling their positions, optimism feels like naivety. Your co-workers, your friends, the media, everything piles on that this time is different, that you need to act now before it's too late.

It takes tremendous faith in the future to do nothing when everything in you wants to react. But doing nothing, just staying the course, is usually the most profitable thing you can do if you're already well-positioned in your investment portfolio.

Some advisors will lead you to believe that their most significant value lies in investment selection or stock picks. In reality, the most significant value a good advisor provides is behavioral counseling and financial planning, keeping you from sabotaging yourself when emotions run high.

A Vanguard study[6] showed that having an advisor adds about 3 percent annually to returns, not from better investments but from helping you have better investing behavior and providing financial planning and tax strategy. Three percent might not sound like much, but compounded over thirty years, it can be the difference between $1 million and over $2 million in retirement assets. That could be the cost of just one big mistake.

I'm not a stock picker. I'm not a market timer. I'm a coach helping you finish the race without regrets.

Every time you stay invested through a market drop,

---

6 Francis M. Kinniry Jr. et al., "Putting a Value on Your Value: Quantifying Vanguard Advisor's Alpha" (Valley Forge, PA: Vanguard, July 2022), https://advisors.vanguard.com/content/dam/fas/pdfs/IARCQAA.pdf

you become a better investor because you built confidence in your ability to endure discomfort. Each time you stay invested through a downturn, the next one feels a little less catastrophic.

Many of you reading this book have lived through catastrophes like the dot-com bubble bursting, the Great Financial Crisis, COVID-19, and other "end of the world" moments. And we will live through many more. Each one felt terrible. Each one felt different. Each one had smart people explaining why this time really was the big one.

And each time, patient investors were rewarded while fearful investors were hurt.

You have a choice to make, not once but every time markets get scary. You can let fear drive your decisions, selling when everyone else is selling, or piling into the one investment everyone else already bought. The better option is to acknowledge the fear of loss or fear of missing out, feel it fully, and stay the course anyway. Even better, you start looking at market corrections as opportunities to buy more shares of companies at a discount.

The first path feels safer in the moment but leads to poorer results. The second path feels scary in the moment, but it leads to wealth and the achievement of your financial goals.

I can't make that choice for you. No advisor can. We can support you, prepare you, and remind you of your plan. But ultimately, you have to choose courage over comfort.

The good news is that you don't have to be perfectly fearless. I've been doing this for fourteen years, and I still feel fear. The difference is that I've learned to act on my plan instead of my fear.

You can learn that, too.

If you stay connected to what you know is true and important to you, you don't separate from what matters most when things are in disarray. You don't disown your values or your goals.

In the next chapter, we'll talk about building a portfolio that can weather any storm. Understanding fear is only half the battle. The other half is having a strategy built for the long haul.

The path through fear isn't around it. It's through it.

CHAPTER 4

BUILDING YOUR FEARLESS PORTFOLIO

In college wrestling, we had a saying, "Drill until it becomes second nature." The wrestler who practices the same takedown a thousand times usually beats the one who tries to land the one big move. Same with investing. A simple, disciplined approach usually beats a big bet on a single speculative investment.

Brian[7] was an engineer in his early sixties when he first came to see me. He'd been laid off and suddenly found himself fully retired earlier than planned.

---

7 Names and details have been changed to protect privacy. This example is for educational purposes only and does not represent any specific client or guarantee results.

"I've been reading that I should put 60 percent of my money in bonds now," he told me at our first meeting. "That's the rule, right? Your age equals your bond percentage?"

I asked him what he wanted retirement to look like. His eyes lit up when he talked about travel. He and his wife had just completed a custom trailer build for a trip to Canada. They had goals of seeing the Arctic Ocean, maybe even flying to Iceland. They wanted to help their parents relocate closer and to pass down an inheritance to their kids. They had dreams, plans, and decades of life left to live.

"So, tell me," I said, "why would you structure your investments like you're planning to die in the next few years when at least one of you might easily live another thirty years?"

He looked confused. "But what if there's a recession? What if the market drops 30 or 40 percent? I can't recover from that now. I need to preserve what I have."

This is a conversation I often have with those nearing retirement. Smart, successful people who have saved and invested diligently suddenly get scared at precisely the moment they should stay brave.

THE FOUR BUCKETS

I brought Brian back to basics. Throughout history, there have been four main categories to allocate funds.

Stocks give you ownership in companies that can grow, pay a dividend, innovate, and raise prices with inflation.

Bonds are IOUs that pay interest but, historically, have lower real returns than equities in the long term.

Commodities, like gold, produce nothing but can make people feel secure, especially during times of global turmoil. Over the long run, gold trails the annual average return of both stocks and bonds.

Cash is most likely to have a negative real return after accounting for inflation, but it's there when you need it.

Digital assets like Bitcoin are a new investment type, and an argument can be made that it's a fifth category. We shall see how it plays out.

For most people building or preserving wealth, the question that really matters when building an investment portfolio is what percentage goes into stocks versus bonds?

I explained to Brian that he already owned plenty of bond-like assets. His Social Security was essentially a government bond. He had a small pension from an earlier job, basically a corporate bond. His home equity was stable and paid off. Add those up, and he already had about two-thirds of his net worth in stable, fixed-income-like assets before buying a single bond fund with his retirement assets. "How about we diversify into growth-focused equities with the remaining retirement investment assets, which make up only about a third of your net worth?" I asked.

AGE-BASED RULES COULD LEAVE YOU FEELING BROKE

The rule Brian had read about, your bond percentage equaling your age, was created when people retired in their sixties and often also passed away in their sixties. Now we retire in our sixties and could very likely live into our nineties and beyond. Three decades of inflation could wreak havoc on a bond-heavy fixed-income portfolio.

"Are you planning to die next year?" I asked Brian.

He laughed. "I hope not."

I ran the numbers with him. Given his monthly expenses, travel desires, and inheritance goals, a conservative portfolio full of fixed-income investments gave him a much lower chance of reaching his long-term goals. Staying growth oriented with his retirement funds increased his chances of achieving his lifetime income goal dramatically. It also meant he had a better chance of reaching his goal of leaving a meaningful inheritance behind for his children and grandchildren.

The choice wasn't between safety and risk. It was between temporary discomfort from volatility experienced in investing in equities versus permanent purchasing power erosion but a smoother ride from investing in fixed-income investments (bonds).

CASH BUFFER FUND STRATEGY

"But what about when the market crashes?" Brian asked. "I've seen it happen. I lived through the Great Recession of 2008. I remember how scary it felt."

This is where my approach may differ from other investors and advisors. Instead of mixing in a bunch of bonds or fixed-income funds into the portfolio to balance it, I wanted Brian to build in what I call a cash-equivalent buffer fund, completely separate from his growth-focused equity-based investments. Two to three years or more worth of his estimated living expenses in cash, high-yield savings accounts, or money market funds. Not invested in stock market-based funds. Not fluctuating. Just sitting there, boring, safe, and earning interest.

"When the market drops 40 percent or more and portfolios decline, knowing lifestyle expenses can be funded for years without selling your retirement investments at a market bottom provides psychological relief," I explained, "you need to know you can fund your lifestyle for years without selling your investment positions at a market bottom while waiting for the market to retreat from its lows. This psychological buffer is more powerful than a bond mutual fund or ETF allocation since bond funds can still decline in a market rout. It lets you stay aggressive with the rest of your investments to reach your stated goals because you have years' worth of stable cash-equivalent reserves to spend down when markets get ugly."

Brian called it his "permission to stay invested" account. He could watch his growth portfolio drop without panicking because he knew he didn't need to touch it for years if needed.

Mike, the coffee shop owner I told you about earlier, demonstrated this principle during the pandemic. When both his business income and investment portfolio crashed simultaneously in March 2020, his business and personal cash reserves allowed him to weather the storm without selling investments at the bottom. He could handle the immediate business challenges while his portfolio recovered naturally over time.

WHAT HISTORY SHOWS

People often ask me what they should expect from different types of investments over time. The answer comes from looking backward, not forward.

According to Jeremy J. Siegel's *Stocks for the Long Run*[8], which analyzes two hundred years of market data, the long-term real return (after inflation) of stocks averages a little less than 7 percent annually. Long-term government bonds deliver between 3 and 4 percent. Gold returns around 1 percent per year after inflation. Cash in a bank account has a negative real return.

These aren't predictions. They're measurements of what actually happened over two centuries. Through world wars, pandemics, depressions, and every crisis you can imagine, owning publicly traded stocks has delivered nearly twice the real return of owning bonds.

This is why Brian needed to stay growth-oriented. A 7 percent real return nearly doubles his purchasing power every ten years. A 4 percent return takes around seventeen years. Over a thirty-year retirement, that difference is massive. It can be the difference between leaving a legacy for your children and having to reduce your standard of living in your later years.

---

8 Jeremy J. Siegel, *Stocks for the Long Run: The Definitive Guide to Financial Market Returns & Long-Term Investment Strategies*, 6th ed. (New York: McGraw Hill, 2022).

The numbers don't guarantee the future will match the past. But they explain why advisors who understand history help clients stay in diversified equity-based investments through a multi-decade retirement despite the volatility. The long-term math is just too compelling to ignore.

FIVE PRINCIPLES

- ASSET ALLOCATION DRIVES RETURNS
- DIVERSIFY WITHIN EACH CATEGORY
- REBALANCE CONSISTENTLY
- REINVEST DIVIDENDS
- STAY GROWTH-ORIENTED LONGER

THE REBALANCING DISCIPLINE

Every year, we rebalance client portfolios back to their original target allocations. If small cap stocks have run up to, say, 25 percent of your portfolio when the original target allocation was 20 percent, for example, we sell the excess and buy whatever's down in the portfolio model.

"Why would I sell my winners to buy losers?" Brian asked when I first explained this.

I replied, "You're selling what's become expensive to buy what's become cheap. You're enforcing the discipline of sticking to a diversified portfolio. You're sticking to a plan."

Think of it like driving on a winding mountain road. You can't control the curves, but you can control your position. Rebalancing keeps you centered in your lane, regardless of which way the market turns.

A SIMPLE PORTFOLIO THAT WORKS

After working with lots of families, after many mistakes and successes, here's an example of an investment portfolio structure that has purpose and simplicity.

For the growth-oriented portion of your investments, for example, a diversified portfolio of equities can be split up between US Large and Small companies, International and Emerging Markets, and Global Real Estate ETFs.

For the stability portion, you can use a separate multi-year cash-equivalent buffer fund in a money market or high-yield savings account that can cover multiple years of your estimated lifestyle costs.

Notice what's missing? No covered call options strategy. No leveraged ETFs. No private equity funds. No market timing tactics. No black box algorithmic trading schemes claiming to give you all the upside and none of the downside.

Just basic, diversified equity index funds that own thousands of the most profitable companies around the world and a cash-equivalent buffer that doesn't fluctuate with the stock market. The cash buffer fund can provide income for multiple years of estimated lifestyle expenses, if needed. A handful of diversified low-cost, equity-based funds that help you beat inflation and an interest-paying money market fund buffer for safety. That's it.

GROWTH MINDSET

Remember the three jars I mentioned making for my kids? Give, spend, and grow? The "grow" jar teaches that money not growing is eroding in purchasing power due to inflation each year.

When someone keeps hundreds of thousands of dollars, over and above their cash reserve goal, in a bank savings account earning next to nothing in interest, they're not being safe. They're succumbing to the loss of purchasing power due to inflation. It's like refusing to maintain your house because repairs feel expensive, then watching it slowly fall apart.

Growing takes faith. Faith that companies will keep innovating. Faith that problems will keep getting solved. Faith that human creativity and the entrepreneurial spirit hasn't peaked.

That faith has rewarded the US stock market investor for over two hundred years, through depressions, stagflation, high inflation, oil shocks, and financial panics.

BRIAN'S TRANSFORMATION

We built Brian's portfolio using these same principles. Most of his money went into low-cost, diversified index ETFs. We set up a multi-year buffer fund he could draw from without touching his investments. We scheduled annual rebalancing.

Three years later, Brian's portfolio has helped him achieve his goals. He's been withdrawing funds each year to supplement his lifestyle, to travel to Alaska, to help his mother-in-law relocate closer to him and his wife, to help his adult children when needed, and to live the retirement he'd hoped for.

His wife had wanted to pay off their mortgage. It was a goal that weighed on her. When we looked at the numbers together, I showed them something encouraging. Based on the gains alone in their retirement accounts, not touching principal, they could pay off their remaining mortgage three times over if they wanted to recognize the gains and pay the capital gains taxes.

"We could be mortgage-free anytime we want," she said, staring at the numbers. "I was beginning to think it wouldn't happen."

When the market dropped 20 percent during the tariff meltdown in the spring of 2025, Brian didn't call me to share panic or worry. He understood. He'd seen his money-market buffer-fund sitting there, ready if needed. He'd seen multiple years of expenses covered. He knew the plan.

"I get it now," he told me. "The drops are just part of it. We stay the course and stay invested."

YOUR IMPLEMENTATION BLUEPRINT

1. CALCULATE YOUR BUFFER FUND

Add up your annual expenses. Multiply by two or three, or more if you want to be even more conservative. This goes into a money market fund or a high yield savings account, insulated from stock market fluctuations.

2. ASSESS YOUR EXISTING STABILITY

Add up your Social Security income, pension income, home equity, and any other stable assets.

3. UTILIZE LOW-COST, DIVERSIFIED, EQUITY-BASED FUNDS FOR THE GROWTH PORTION OF YOUR PORTFOLIO

Common equity fund categories: US Large Cap, US Small Cap, International Developed Markets, Emerging Markets, and Global Real Estate.
A handful of ETFs or index funds can provide complete diversification.

4. REBALANCE CONSISTENTLY AND REINVEST DIVIDENDS

Rebalance your portfolio on the same date every year. Reinvest your dividends each quarter to help bring your portfolio back to its original allocation percentages.

THE BOTTOM LINE

Building the portfolio is the easy part. The hard part is leaving it alone when fear or greed starts to kick in.

When markets drop by half, your simple portfolio won't need tinkering with. Your buffer fund will keep you from having to sell. Your dividend reinvesting discipline will cause you to buy when everyone else is selling.

When markets soar, and it seems like everyone is getting rich on the latest investment fad, your fundamentally sound portfolio will keep chugging along, building real wealth while others chase moonshot returns in over-concentrated positions. A fearless portfolio isn't fearless because it avoids risk. It's fearless because it's built to withstand whatever markets throw at it without requiring you to predict the future or time your moves perfectly.

A simplified portfolio with low-cost publicly traded equity funds. Broad diversification across different fund categories. Reinvest Dividends. Rebalance consistently. Patience and discipline. Faith in the future. These are long-term wealth-building principles that work regardless of who's president, what the Fed does, or where the economy's headed.

You won't have a thrilling story about the killing you made on a hot stock. But in twenty years, while the market-timing investors are still trying to get back to even, you'll be on your way to being financially free.

In the next chapter, we'll talk about what happens when you suddenly have more money than you ever imagined. Because while losing money is scary, suddenly having millions can be paralyzing in its own way.

CHAPTER 5

WINDFALLS, INHERITANCES, AND LIFE-CHANGING MONEY

THREE YEARS HAD PASSED since Mary[9] lost her father to a motor vehicle incident. Three years of lawyers, court dates, and waiting. When she first walked into my office she was thirty-one living with a roommate. The settlement was supposed to be coming, $3 million from a wrongful death claim, but it still felt hypothetical to her.

"I hope it's coming," she told me in that first meeting.

9 Names and details have been changed to protect privacy. This example is for educational purposes only and does not represent any specific client or guarantee results.

"The lawyers keep saying soon. But even if it does, I have no idea what to do with it. I feel uneducated about all this."

Mary found me online while searching for a fiduciary financial advisor. She did research because she wanted someone who would teach her, not just sell her products. Someone who would help her make sure this money, which came from the worst thing that ever happened to her family, would last her a lifetime.

The thing about windfalls is that the money often comes wrapped in grief, guilt, or a sense of disorientation. It arrives when you're least equipped to handle it, emotionally. And everyone suddenly has opinions about what you should do with it.

THE WEIGHT OF SUDDEN WEALTH

When someone receives a large sum of money unexpectedly, the first emotion isn't usually joy. It's paralysis.

"I don't want to do the wrong thing, so I'm doing nothing," one client told me. He'd inherited $500,000 from his parents, and it had been sitting in a checking account for two years, earning almost no interest. The fear of making a mistake was costing him thousands in lost growth potential, but that felt safer than risking losing money.

This paralysis makes sense. Most people spend decades gradually accumulating wealth. They learn as they go, make small mistakes, and build confidence over time. But when wealth arrives all at once, there's no learning curve. The stakes feel impossibly high.

Mary felt this acutely. "I've driven beater cars my whole life," she said. "Now I'm supposed to know what to do with millions?"

THE FIRST NINETY DAYS

By our second meeting, Mary's settlement had arrived. We laid out a plan that started with breathing room, not big decisions.

First, we paid off her debts. Credit cards and student loans. The psychological relief of being debt-free can't be overstated. It clears your mind to make better long-term decisions.

Second, we set aside her dream car fund. She'd always wanted a specific full-size SUV. Some advisors would say this is frivolous, but I disagree. After years of sacrifice and now loss, doing something purely for joy helps people believe the money is real and that it's okay to benefit from it.

Third, we created a cash reserve in a separate interest-earning savings account to give her some time and space before making big life decisions. This removed the pressure to figure everything out immediately. She could keep working, keep living normally, and take time to adjust to her new reality.

Only after these immediate needs were met did we start to build a plan for long-term investing.

THE EDUCATION COMPONENT

Mary had been clear from the beginning. "I want to learn more. I want to understand what I'm doing with this money."

This hunger for education is also common among windfall recipients. They know the weight of what they've been given and want to be worthy stewards of it. But the financial industry often responds by making things more complex and rushed, not clearer and calmer.

I took the opposite approach. We spent hours just talking through basics. What's a stock? What's a bond? Why do markets go up and down? How does inflation work?

"No one ever explained this stuff," Mary told me after one session. "They just expected me to know or made it seem too complicated to understand, which made me feel dumb."

THE UNIQUE CHALLENGES OF DIFFERENT WINDFALLS

Not all windfalls are the same. Each type brings its own emotional and practical challenges.

Inheritance from parents often comes with guilt about benefiting from their death and pressure to honor their memory through perfect decisions. I've worked with children who couldn't bring themselves to sell their father's individual stocks because it felt like betrayal, even when those positions didn't fit their plan, and they weren't expected to hold them forever.

Settlements like Mary's carry the weight of trauma. The money is forever linked to loss. There's also often family dynamics involved, with siblings or other relatives who also received settlements making different choices.

Business sales bring a different challenge. After decades of pouring everything into a company, entrepreneurs struggle to transition from active income to passive investing. One client who sold his construction company for $4.5 million kept wanting to "do something more" with the money. The idea of just letting it sit in diversified stock funds felt like laziness after a lifetime of hustle.

Retirement rollovers might seem less emotional, but they carry their own burden. Someone with $2 million in a 401(k) invested in company stock suddenly must make financial decisions with wealth that didn't seem real to them at first. It was just numbers on a statement for twenty years, and now it's time to create a lifetime stream of income with it. One client said, "It just felt like monopoly money before I had to start strategizing retirement withdrawals from it."

THE SHARKS CIRCLE

When word gets out that you have money, and it always does, the sharks start circling.

Banks have triggers that flag large deposits. Suddenly, you're getting calls from their wealth management department. Financial services salespeople materialize with complicated products that promise to protect your newfound wealth. Family members have business opportunities. Friends have real estate development ideas.

Mary experienced all of this. "People I hadn't talked to in years suddenly wanted to catch up," she said. "And they all had their own financial opinions or wanted something."

This is where having an advisor becomes a shield. When someone approaches you with a can't-miss investment opportunity, you can simply say, "I'll run it by my advisor." It's easier than saying no directly, and it puts a professional barrier between you and a high-pressure decision.

BUILDING THE WINDFALL PORTFOLIO

For Mary, we built a three-bucket approach that I use with windfall recipients.

Bucket One: The "sleep at night" fund. Two to three years of living expenses in money market funds, completely separate from investments. This removes the fear that a market crash could force you back to your old lifestyle or worse.

Bucket Two: Medium-term goals. For Mary, this included a down payment on a future home and the potential to own a caregiving business. This money went into a fixed-income heavy portfolio, earning interest but accessible.

Bucket Three: Long-term wealth. This is the serious money, invested for growth because Mary has decades ahead of her. We set up a monthly distribution from this account to her checking account, starting at a few thousand dollars and increasing it over time as needed. This created a paycheck supplement that gave her time and financial margin before making career moves. She could make big lifestyle changes when she felt ready.

THE PERMISSION TO LIVE

Contrary to popular belief, one of the hardest things for some windfall recipients is permitting themselves to use the money. They've often lived frugally for so long that spending feels wrong, even dangerous.

"What if I run out?" Mary asked me constantly in the early days. "What if I blow it all?"

We addressed this by creating "permission buckets." This is money specifically designated for enjoyment. For Mary, this meant travel goals with specific dollar amounts attached. A concert trip to Montreal with friends. A family visit in NYC. Two weeks in Japan next year.

These aren't frivolous splurges. They're planned expenditures that fit within the overall strategy. But psychologically having permission to enjoy the money without guilt is transformative.

THE LONG VIEW

A year after our first meeting, Mary is a different person. Not because the money changed her personality but because the fear of making a big mistake is gone.

"I don't feel uneducated anymore," she told me recently. "I understand what we're doing and why. When the market took a dive in April, I didn't panic. I knew we had planned for this."

Her portfolio has grown despite market volatility. She's traveled to places she'd only dreamed of. She's helped friends' children with gifts for college expenses. Most importantly, she's living without the constant anxiety that marked those first months after receiving the settlement payout.

WHEN YOU'RE NOT READY

Not everyone who receives a windfall is ready to make decisions. I met with a woman whose father had been a barber. She inherited his shop along with other assets. Every time she walked into his shop, the smells transported her back to childhood. The thought of selling it was unbearable.

"I don't think I'm ready," she said in our second meeting.

"That's perfectly okay," I told her. "There's no rule that says you have to make decisions within a certain amount of time."

Sometimes the best advice is to wait because grief has its own timeline. Rushing financial decisions because someone says you should is a recipe for regret.

THE BOTTOM LINE ON WINDFALLS

If you've received or might receive a windfall, here's what helps:

First, you have permission to take your time. The money won't disappear if you don't invest it immediately. It's better to move slowly and deliberately than to rush into decisions you're not ready to make. You can always store the funds in a secure and reputable FDIC or SIPC-insured bank account or brokerage account until you're ready.

Second, education matters. Becoming a financial expert isn't necessary, but understanding what's happening with your money is important. If an advisor can't explain something in a way that you can fully understand, they may not be a good fit for you.

Third, the emotional challenges are often harder than the financial ones. Grief, guilt, fear, and family dynamics don't disappear just because you have money. Sometimes they get worse. But having a financial plan simplifies decision-making.

Fourth, a team helps. Beyond an advisor, consider a CPA for taxes, an attorney for estate planning, and possibly a therapist for emotional and mental support.

Finally, remember that this money, however it came to you, is an opportunity to live according to your values. Whether that's providing meaningful experiences for your family, pursuing work that is fulfilling to you, or being generous to causes and people you care about.

Let your values, not your fears, guide your decisions. Sudden wealth events happen often in the US. Every day, someone receives money that could change their life. The difference between those who thrive and those who struggle isn't intelligence or education. It's having the right support, the right plan, and the patience to let both develop over time.

Your windfall doesn't have to be a burden. With the right approach, it can be the foundation for the life you've always wanted to live.

CHAPTER 6

WHY GOING IT ALONE IS RISKY BUSINESS

WHEN I WAS THIRTY years old, sitting in that Burger King parking lot during my first panic attack, I kept thinking, *"I'm alone with this. No one can help me. I have to figure this out on my own. I don't know what to do."*

The feeling of aloneness made everything worse. The physical symptoms were terrifying enough, but the loneliness amplified the fear.

Eventually, I learned that I didn't have to face those moments alone. I shared my fears with my wife and my friends. I worked with experts in neuroscience. I built a network of support so that when panic started rising, I had people and tools to help me through it. It was hard work, especially at the beginning.

The same principle applies to investing. The path is hard enough on its own. Trying to walk it completely alone makes it really tough.

THE ILLUSION OF SELF-SUFFICIENCY

There's something admirable about self-reliance. I get it. You've built a successful career or business largely on your own merit. You're intelligent. You can analyze reports. You can research. Why would you need someone else to help manage your money?

I meet people all the time who've been researching investments for years, but still haven't made any meaningful progress in their wealth-building journey. They're waiting for one more piece of information, one more article, one more podcast that will finally give them the confidence to invest in a portfolio and stick with it.

That confidence rarely comes because the research is infinite. There's always another perspective to consider, another risk to evaluate, another strategy to explore. The deluge of information available becomes the obstacle.

THE ACCOUNTABILITY FACTOR

What I've learned about human nature is that we're exceptionally good at having the best of intentions but quite bad at following through on them.

You know you shouldn't check your investment accounts every day during market volatility. But how many times have you logged in anyway, just to stress yourself out with information that doesn't change your long-term plan?

You know you should increase your retirement contributions as your income grows. Do you, or does the money quietly disappear into lifestyle inflation?

Having an advisor creates external accountability. Not because you can't understand these concepts yourself, but because knowing someone will follow up with your progress changes your behavior.

One client told me, "I know all this stuff intellectually. I've read the books. I understand diversification and long-term thinking. But when I talk with you during a market crash and you say things like, 'Remember why we built this portfolio. Or, we are properly invested based on your goals.' It helps me more than reading it on a screen."

THE COST OF ISOLATION DURING CRISIS

The real test of going it alone isn't during the good times. It's during the crashes.

In March of 2020, I spent my days on the phone with clients. Not giving them new information or adjusting their portfolios. Just being present. Asking them how they are doing. Listening to their concerns and fears. Reminding them of what they already knew but needed to hear from another human being.

"We planned for this. Your buffer fund has you covered for years. Things will get better. I'm not sure when or how, but it will. Another world-ending event will come along, and patient investors will continue to be rewarded."

Those weren't magic words. They were the same things we'd discussed in previous meetings. But hearing them from someone who wasn't panicking, someone who'd walked through multiple market crashes, made the difference between staying invested and selling at the bottom.

Try to be that voice for yourself when you're terrified or upset. Try to access your rational brain when your primitive survival instincts are sounding the alarm. It's a tall order.

THE SECOND OPINION VALUE

Even if you're confident in your investment knowledge, there's value in having someone review your blind spots.

I've met with plenty of people who were doing fine on their own. They had a logical portfolio of investments, reasonable allocations, and adequate reserves. But in our conversation, we'd discover one or two things they hadn't considered.

Maybe they didn't know about a tax savings strategy in their business, like setting up a retirement plan. Maybe they didn't know about donor-advised funds, which allow them to give charitably and eliminate taxes on capital gains. Maybe they simply were holding too much cash in a bank account earning almost zero interest, when they could build a proper cash reserve fund earning ten times or more in interest.

These might not be major mistakes, but they're opportunities. Sometimes just having someone confirm you're on the right track provides peace of mind that's hard to quantify but genuinely valuable.

One couple came to me after managing their own investments for fifteen years. "We're doing okay," they said. "But we don't know if we're doing *enough*. We have nothing to compare it to except what we read online, and everyone online seems to be either making a killing or going bankrupt."

We reviewed their portfolio. Their investments were logical. They were making retirement account contributions. They just needed someone with experience to confirm they were on track.

"That conversation was worth it just for the confidence in what we're doing," the husband told me six months later. "We stopped continually second-guessing ourselves."

WHEN DIY MAKES SENSE

Not everyone needs or wants a formal financial advisory relationship.

If your situation is straightforward, if you have the discipline to stay invested through downturns, if you're not burdened by the weight of investment decisions, or if you have the time and interest to manage it yourself, you can absolutely do this on your own.

There are excellent resources available. Low-cost index funds make investing simple. Automatic 401(k) contributions make disciplined saving easier. If you're the kind of person who can set a strategy and stick with it regardless of what markets do, you can be just fine going solo. There are plenty of do-it-yourself investors out there.

The question isn't whether you're smart enough.

The question is more along the lines of whether or not you want someone to partner with on a financial strategy and to delegate proactive financial upkeep to.

There comes a point when trying to go it alone costs you more than hiring help would.

THE COST OF GOOD ADVICE

The financial services industry has done an extraordinary job of confusing people about cost.

A commissioned salesperson might charge you nothing out of pocket but embed a 5 percent or more fee in the product they sell you, plus ongoing fees you never see. An advisor charging around 1 percent of assets under management may seem unnecessary until you realize they're saving you from behavioral investing mistakes that could cost more.

Fee-only advisors charge transparently. You pay for advice, not for products. The typical cost runs between one and one and a half percent of assets managed annually, depending on complexity and service level.

Is that worth it?

It depends on your situation and how much you would value having a financial decision-making partner. Working with a financial advisor gives you someone to talk you out of panic selling during crashes and to keep you diversified during a market bubble. Someone to remind you of your values when fear or FOMO strikes. Someone to handle the annual maintenance you know you should do, but may procrastinate on it. Someone to help with tax planning before the end of the year, especially if you're a business owner. Someone who's thinking about your financial situation even when you're not.

WHAT TO LOOK FOR IN AN ADVISOR

If you decide you want guidance, here's what matters:

HOW TO CHOOSE A FINANCIAL ADVISOR

FEE-ONLY, FIDUCIARY

This means they're legally required to act in your best interest and are compensated by fees you pay directly, not by commissions on product sales.

CFP® CERTIFICATION

It shows they've met education requirements, passed comprehensive exams, and committed to ongoing education and ethical standards.

EXPERIENCE WITH YOUR SITUATION

If you received an inheritance, you want someone who's helped others navigate windfalls. If you're a business owner, find someone who regularly works with business owners.

CLEAR COMMUNICATION

If they can't explain their philosophy in plain language, keep looking. Complexity is often a smoke screen. Your gut feeling goes a long way. You want to feel comfortable having conversations with whoever you choose to work with.

VALUES ALIGNMENT

If faith guides your life decisions, you want an advisor who can relate to that. If generosity matters to you, find someone who helps clients give strategically. You'll be talking about deeply personal topics. Chemistry matters.

THE LONELINESS OF MAJOR DECISIONS

My grandmother made financial decisions on her own because she wanted to keep things private. She didn't want to burden anyone. She thought she could figure things out on her own.

That privacy and lack of financial education were costly.

I think about this whenever someone tells me they don't need help. Maybe they don't. But the question isn't whether you're capable. The question is whether doing it yourself is actually serving you well.

Major financial decisions made in isolation carry more risk. Not because of a lack of intelligence but because of a narrowed perspective. It's tough to see your own blind spots. It's tough to be objective about your own financial worries. It's tough to talk yourself down when panic or greed sets in.

Some paths are safer with company. Not because you're weak but because the terrain is treacherous and having someone who's walked it before increases your odds of reaching your destination on time and in one piece.

You can *try* to be the still, small voice for yourself. Some people can. But most of us need to hear it from someone else, someone who isn't consumed by the same fear, someone who's been through this before and knows how it has played out historically.

THE FREEDOM TO CHOOSE

Some journeys benefit from a guide. You can climb a fourteen-thousand-foot mountain alone. People do it. But you're more likely to reach the summit if you're with someone who knows the trail, who can point out the dangerous sections, who can encourage you when you want to turn back. And maybe most importantly, make sure you're prepared before you even start the journey.

The sheer cliff sides will still be there. The risks will still be real. Markets will still drop. Fear will still rise up. Distractions will still be present. The question is whether you want to face those challenges alone or with someone in your corner who's been through it before.

For some people, going solo works. For others, having a trusted advisor makes the journey easier and more likely to succeed. Not to mention, more fun and relaxed.

Whatever you choose, take some time to make a deliberate decision.

In the next chapter, we'll explore what it means to live your values through your wealth. Because having the right strategies and the right support only matters if they serve what matters most to you.

CHAPTER 7

LIVING YOUR VALUES THROUGH YOUR WEALTH

"I WANT TO BE remembered as faithful and generous, not as just a rich guy."

A client said this to me, and it made me stop and think. Many people don't connect their money to how they want to be remembered until it's too late. They accumulate wealth without considering what it's all really for.

Successful professionals who've done most things right to get to where they are often feel empty about it. They have the accounts, the portfolio, and the cash. But when I ask what it's all for, they sometimes don't have a good answer.

BALANCING THE FOUR SQUARES

One framework I use with clients is what I call the Four Squares of Faith, Family, Health, and Wealth. The reality is it's really tough to be at a hundred percent in all four simultaneously. When I'm hyper-focused on health, something else falls by the wayside. When business demands spike, family or wellness takes a hit.

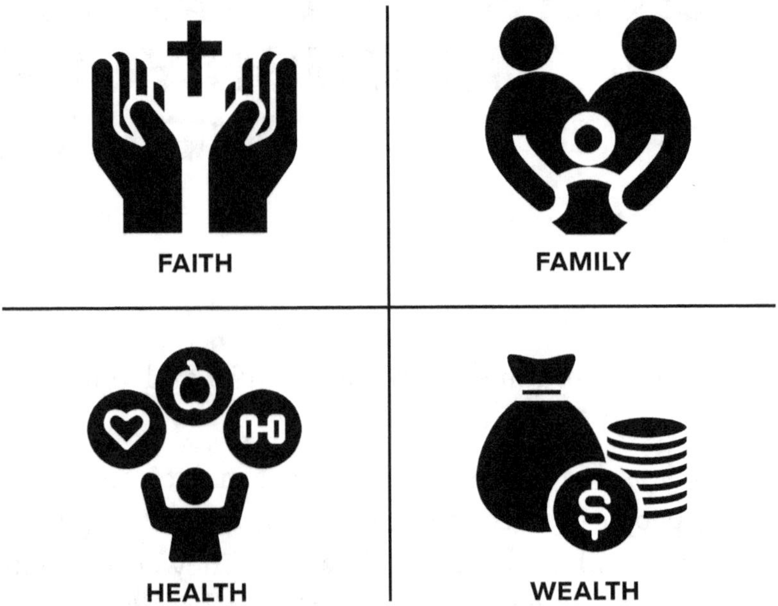

The goal is awareness. When one square gets too much attention for too long, the others suffer in ways you'll eventually regret.

For Mark and Erin[10], my married nurse practitioner clients, this framework helped them articulate what wasn't working. They were highly focused on their career (wealth) but felt low about their personal wellness. They felt successful but exhausted and unmotivated.

"Do you have a retirement age in mind?" I asked.

They looked at each other. They'd been wrestling with this question.

"We've always talked about doing international missions work someday," Mark said. "Using our skills to provide healthcare in places that really need it. But we figured that was something for our sixties or beyond, after we'd fully retired."

"What if you could do that in your forties instead?" I asked.

Their eyes lit up. This wasn't something they'd considered possible. We ran the numbers and found that if they maintained their savings rate and stayed disciplined, it was entirely achievable. They could set up accessible accounts to fund this dream without early withdrawal penalties.

Building a "Freedom Fund" created options to rebalance those squares in their forties, rather than waiting until their sixties, when their health might not cooperate.

---

10 Names and details have been changed to protect privacy. This example is for educational purposes only and does not represent any specific client or guarantee results.

Money aligned with your values means you can make intentional choices about where to focus your energy.

For the first time, their money had direction beyond simply saving and working more.

BUILDING THE FREEDOM FUND

We opened a new joint taxable investment account for them to add monthly income into, in addition to their retirement account contributions. This money is accessible and penalty-free at any age. They still have to plan for taxes on capital gains transactions or incoming dividends. However, they can use these funds in their forties and fifties as a freedom fund and a missions work fund without being restricted by age limits or withdrawal penalties applicable to retirement accounts.

This created peace. Not just peace about the future but peace about the present. They could work diligently now and then have the option to serve in international missions work, providing health care to people in hard-to-reach places.

They're both still working. They're both committed professionals. But now they have a pathway to something that was just a dream before. Now they are taking steps toward making it a reality. They have a new focus and renewed motivation for working.

We also started giving to charities they cared about, now, from their investments. They started giving appreciated shares of investment funds from their taxable investment account to their donor-advised fund (DAF). This allowed them to receive a tax deduction for charitable gifts now while investing some of those funds for future giving and giving some away to several nonprofit organizations now.

Instead of giving cash, we identified appreciated stock in their taxable account that they held for over a year and donated those shares. This accomplished two things. First, they avoided capital gains taxes on the appreciation. Second, it helped them to be intentional about their giving. Every quarter, we determine how much they want to give, and we transfer shares of investments that have appreciated over the last year or longer.

"It's changed how we think about money," Mark told me. "It's not just ours to keep. It's ours to steward."

WORK OPTIONAL, NOT WORK FREE

Financial independence doesn't mean you have to stop working altogether. It means working by choice, not by default. It means doing work you wouldn't want to stop, even if you had the option to financially. Doing work based on your calling and skills, work that you feel fulfilled by and uniquely suited to do based on your strengths. And it helps that the income generated supports your family and provides extra to give and invest.

This is what we're building toward with Mark and Erin. Not a traditional retirement at age sixty-seven when you stop contributing your talents to people who need them, but a work-optional life where you do meaningful work to serve others because you want to.

I think about this in my own practice. I get to help lots of families reach their most cherished financial goals in ways that utilize my strengths and my calling to help others. As the owner of my firm, I can be deliberate in how many new clients I take on, which allows me to prioritize getting to know each client personally and spend unhurried time with them when they need me. The income is necessary, of course. But being able to do it in a way that energizes me and motivates me to keep improving year after year is the real blessing.

THE INTEGRATION CHALLENGE

One of the most important conversations I have with couples is when their values don't align. Not because they disagree fundamentally but because they haven't actually talked about what drives their financial decisions.

When I work with couples to explore their deeper motivations about money, revelations emerge that surprise even them. One spouse discovers for the first time why the other seems anxious about spending or obsessed with saving.

I remember one couple where the husband insisted on keeping large amounts of cash in a safe at home, even though they had other near-term goals they could use the money for. His wife thought he was being overly cautious, even controlling. But when we dug deeper into his relationship with money, the truth emerged.

"My dad lost his high-paying corporate job when I was in high school," he finally said. "We had to file for bankruptcy six months later. I was old enough to understand what was happening but too young to help. I don't want my kids to feel that burden."

His wife's entire perspective shifted in that moment. What seemed like excessive caution turned out to be love expressed through protection. She wanted to spend more on family experiences while the kids were young. He wanted to save more for family security. They were both expressing love for their children, just through different languages.

Once they understood each other's underlying motivations, they could find balance. They kept his cash fund in place for his confidence but also created a separate "family adventure fund" for her priority of making memories. Both values were honored because both were understood.

This is why I like to make sure both spouses can attend the financial planning meetings. I ask them both what they value and what's important to them. Sometimes they hear things from their spouse that they haven't heard before, which deepens their marital harmony. I like to give space to listen to both of their stories and their financial backgrounds, allowing time for each to share their desires, thoughts, and concerns about their finances.

PRACTICAL WAYS TO ALIGN MONEY WITH VALUES

If family experiences matter most, set up a high yield savings account and nickname it "Family Fun." Add to it monthly and commit to spending it by year-end on trips, adventures, or outings.

Business owners wanting flexibility can fund an "Opportunity Fund" in a brokerage account. Invested for growth but accessible before retirement, giving options when work slows or new business opportunities arise.

For those feeling called to increased generosity, establish a giving fund through a separate savings account or donor-advised fund and set up monthly automated contributions. When someone needs help or a cause stirs your heart, the money is already there. If it's in the account, saying "yes" to whoever may be needing the help becomes much easier.

PERMISSION TO LIVE NOW

Many people need validation to align money with their values, especially when generosity or experiences compete with accumulation.

One couple wanted to fund adoptions for families who couldn't afford them but kept hesitating. "We should probably keep investing for retirement," the husband said. When we confirmed they were on track, I asked simply, "Then why aren't you funding adoptions now?" They couldn't answer. There's always a reason to wait for "enough" before being generous, but the feeling of "enough" often never comes.

Within a year, they'd helped two families adopt babies in need of parents and a home. The joy and fulfillment that brought them was worth more than any investment return. Sometimes my role is simply giving permission to do what people already knew was important. To spend on what matters now. To be generous now rather than someday. To give with a warm hand as opposed to waiting to give an inheritance at death. To use wealth while they can see its impact.

MONEY'S TRUE PURPOSE

If someone retires at sixty-five, they could live another thirty years. That's decades of potential wealth-building that can impact a family's legacy. Add their kids' and grandkids' lifetimes, and decisions made today can span a century.

Money just sitting in cash loses roughly half its purchasing power over thirty years to inflation. But money working in a diversified portfolio of equities that can grow and pay dividends can fund decades of home down- payments, college tuition fees, travel experiences and generosity.

Regret weighs tons. The regret of not keeping up with inflation. The regret of not having the impact you hoped to make. The regret of reaching the end and realizing wealth served no purpose beyond accumulation.

Discipline weighs less than regret, even though it feels harder in the moment.

So start by asking yourself, "What do I want money to do for me?" As opposed to starting with questions like, "What should I invest in? Or, what return percentage can I get?"

What do you want money to *actually* do?

Create financial security for your family? Buy freedom from high-stress or low-fulfillment work? Fund causes that matter to you? Enable experiences with your children? Build a legacy fund for grandkids' college expenses? Make an impact beyond your own lifetime?

Answer that question with clarity, and everything else becomes secondary. The investments, allocations, and strategies are just tools serving a purpose.

Without purpose, wealth is just numbers accumulating toward nothing. Money ought to be used to serve your values.

CONCLUSION

FROM FEAR TO FREEDOM

THE BOOK YOU'VE JUST read isn't really about eliminating all feelings of fear. It's about being able to show courage.

Courage to face your fears when investing in the stock market. Courage to keep things simple when everyone else complicates them. Courage to stay invested when you want to move to cash. Courage to stay diversified when seemingly everyone is piling into the one thing going up the most. Courage to align your wealth with your values.

Most of all, the courage to act despite your fears.

WHAT THIS WORK MEANS

I often think about my grandmother, especially when I meet with clients or prospective clients. Seeing how financial decisions impacted my family, I'm passionate about helping others avoid similar pitfalls, like getting stuck with a bad financial product or just not making the most of their assets. I want to help shield individuals and their loved ones from similar mistakes.

I want to be the still, small voice for my clients when they feel worried or stressed about money and investing.

FROM FEAR TO FREEDOM

I've watched this transformation happen over and over.

One client had closed their local bookkeeping business to retire. As she began planning to move into a retirement living community, she wasn't sure whether she would have any extra funds after paying for basic living expenses to take the fun trips she had dreamed of in retirement. I set up a lifetime income plan with proceeds from the sale of her real estate property. Now she could actually have money to give to her children, which she wanted to do, and have extra money to travel.

"What's the big trip that you want to go on?" I asked her.

She wanted to tour Florence, Italy, and take one of her grandchildren with her. So we put it in writing and set the date. She immediately started to feel freedom, relief, and joy. "Oh, wow, I can set this trip up and go and not feel like I'm going to be forced to stay at home all day, every day."

Another client, a retired teacher, just wants to have something to leave her two daughters when she passes away. She now knows this money will be invested in growth-oriented funds. It's going to make a substantial impact. It could be used to put a down payment on a future home for her kids or to help send her grandkids to college.

What does being able to help people do these types of things mean to me? It's the most important thing I can think of doing. It's fulfilling and energizing. I'm living the career I feel I was made for.

YOUR NEXT STEP

Right now, while this book is fresh in your mind, consider one action that resonates most.

You could start by writing down your goals and values. Then block out an hour each quarter on your calendar to review and assess progress. You could open a high-yield savings account for a cash buffer. You could start funding a retirement account from your business profits. You could reach out to a fee-only, fiduciary CFP® professional if you're curious how they might be able to help.

The details will fall into place once you start. Good enough today beats waiting for perfect someday.

THE CHOICE

You have a choice to make, not once but every time markets take a hit or are in a bubble.

You can let fear drive your decisions, selling when everyone else is selling, or chasing whatever sector has already peaked. Or you can acknowledge the fear, let it pass through you, and stay the course anyway.

The first path feels safer in the moment but leads to worse results. The second feels terrifying but offers a higher chance of building wealth and achieving your goals in the long run.

My grandmother didn't have the guidance she needed. You have what she could have used with a decision-making framework aligned with your values, access to low-cost diversified equity-based ETFs, and the ability to get professional advice when you need it.

What you do with these advantages is up to you.

THE PATH FORWARD

This book is my invitation to stop letting fear steal the wealth and the life you could be building. Start with what matters most. Keep it simple. Stay the course when others flee. Make financial decisions in service of your goals.

If you'd like help implementing this, I'm here. You can reach me through my website or email me directly. But whether you work with me, another advisor, or go it alone, the important thing is that you start.

The capital markets will be there tomorrow, offering the same opportunities they've offered for over two centuries. The only question is whether you'll participate or watch from the sidelines.

Your story doesn't have to end with regret about chances not taken or fear not overcome.

The choice is yours. The time is now.

Take the first step.

ABOUT THE AUTHOR

ERIC MALDONADO, CFP®, MBA, is a fee-only, fiduciary financial advisor and founder of Aquila Wealth Advisors, a registered investment advisory firm, based in San Luis Obispo, CA. With over a decade of experience as a CERTIFIED FINANCIAL PLANNER® professional, Eric specializes in helping individuals and families who have received inheritances, windfalls, or accumulated significant assets navigate the emotional and practical challenges of wealth management.

Eric's path to financial advising was shaped by personal experience. After watching his grandmother lose her fully paid-off home to foreclosure when he was nine years old, he understood firsthand how fear and confusion can lead to regrettable financial decisions. This childhood experience drives his commitment to ensuring others have the guidance and support his grandmother lacked.

Before launching his own firm eight years ago, Eric spent seven years working at an independent financial advisory firm, where he received his CERTIFIED FINANCIAL PLANNER® certification. Frustrated by the conflicts of interest prevalent in the commission- and fee-based areas of financial services, he established his fee-only, fiduciary advisory business where he felt he could fully put clients' interests first.

Eric's background as a Division I college wrestler instilled the discipline and persistence that characterize his investment philosophy. Wrestling is one of the most significant aspects of his life, shaping who he is today. He applies the same principles that brought success in wrestling (consistent practice, staying the course under pressure, and having a good coach) to helping clients build and preserve wealth.

Eric helps clients align their financial decisions with their values, whether rooted in faith or other deeply held principles. He believes that money without meaning is just numbers on a screen, and he works with each client to ensure their wealth serves their unique purpose.

In 2025, Eric returned from a year-long sabbatical with his wife and four children in the Sequoia National Forest, an experience that reinforced his belief in living according to one's values rather than being controlled by fear. The sabbatical, planned and saved for over seven years, demonstrated the very principles he teaches clients by setting meaningful goals, preparing financially, and having the courage to take the leap to do what matters most despite uncertainty.

As a business owner who has navigated market crashes, raised a family, and started a financial planning firm while maintaining his values, Eric brings both professional expertise and personal experience to his work.

He works with business owners and retirees, ensuring he can provide personalized attention and be available when they need guidance most.

When he's not helping clients navigate their financial journeys, he coaches youth sports, maintains his daily journal practice, and continues planning the family's next adventure, which could be Hawaii, Portugal, or Costa Rica for their next family sabbatical in another seven years.

His investment philosophy is simple. Own high-quality companies through low-cost diversified exchange-traded funds, maintain adequate interest-paying cash reserves, stay patient during market downturns and disciplined during market euphoria, and keep your financial decisions aligned with your values. But his real expertise lies in helping clients find the courage to implement and stick with these simple principles when fear tries to derail them.

Eric holds a bachelor's degree in business administration with a concentration in Finance from California Polytechnic State University, San Luis Obispo, CA, and a Master of Business Administration (MBA) degree in Financial Planning from Indiana Wesleyan University.

To learn more about working with Eric or to schedule an introductory conversation, visit:

> **www.AquilaWealth.com**
>
> or email him directly at
>
> **info@aquilawealth.com**

He is available to his clients and prospective clients whenever they need guidance, especially when markets are turbulent and emotions run high.

DISCLAIMER

Advisory services are offered through Aquila Wealth Advisors, LLC dba Aquila Wealth, an investment adviser registered with the state of CA. Advisory services are only offered to clients or prospective clients where Aquila Wealth Advisors, LLC dba Aquila Wealth and its representatives are properly registered or exempt from registration.

The information in this publication is not intended as tax, accounting, or legal advice, nor is it an offer or solicitation to buy or sell, or as an endorsement of any company, security, fund, or other offering. Information provided should not be solely relied upon for decision making. Please consult your legal, tax, or accounting professional regarding your specific situation. Investments involve risk and have the potential for complete loss. It should not be assumed that any recommendations made will necessarily be profitable.

The information in this publication is provided "AS IS" and without warranties either express or implied, and the information may not be free from error. Your use of the information provided is at your sole risk.